The Illustrious Corpse

A non-mystery play by Tariq Ali

Sir Huntley Palmer Jones **Trevor Thomas**
Dr Desdemona Jones **Kristin Milward**
Sir Richard Everall **Russell Dixon**
Ms Andrea Adelard / A Female
Newscaster / Prosecutor **Beverley Longhurst**

Directed by **Iqbal Khan**
Dramaturgy **Nöel Greig** and **Esther Richardson**
Assistant Director **Sarah Chiswell**
Designed by **Kate Unwin**
Lighting by **Miriam Spencer**
Sound by **Ben Harrison**

Production Manager **Graham Lister**
Company Manager **Harriet Roy**
Stage Manager **Fiona H Mott**
Deputy Stage Manager **Sarah Buik**
Assistant Stage Manager **Helen King**
Wardrobe Supervisor **Denise Edwards**

Leicester Haymarket Theatre would like to thank all those involved
in the development of this piece:

Adel Al-Salloum
Alison Carney
Russell Dixon
Paddy Glynn
Trevor H Laird

The Illustrious Corpse was originally commissioned by
Leicestershire County Council

Company

Russell Dixon
Sir Richard Everall

Trained at Bristol Old Vic. Leicester Haymarket credits include Johnnypateenmike in *The Cripple of Inishmaan,* Sergei in *On Your Toes,* Oscar Wilde in *Saint Oscar*, Brack in *Hedda Gabler,* The Reciter in *Pacific Overtures*, Ben in *Follies* and Fredrik *in A Little Night Music*. Other theatre credits include *The Seagull, The Beggar's Opera* (Royal Exchange), *Who's Afraid of Virginia Woolf* (Sheffield Crucible), *King Lear* (in the Nottingham Playhouse production), *Woman in Mind, Neville's Island* (Stephen Joseph Theatre in the Round, Scarborough), *Breaking the Code* (Oldham Coliseum), *Making Tracks* (Greenwich Theatre), *Cabaret* (Derby Playhouse), *'Tis a Pity She's a Whore* (Royal National Theatre), *Pericles, The Duchess of Malfi, Moscow Gold* (RSC), *A Chorus of Disapproval* (Lyric Theatre*), Iolanthe* (Sadlers Wells Theatre). Russell is a frequent broadcaster on Radio 3 and 4. Television credits include *Coronation Street, The Vice, Peak Practice, Kavanagh QC, Bugs, Heartbeat, Dalziel and Pascoe* and *Fat Friends*. Films include Father Ryan in *Liam*, Dr. Quinton in *The Emperor's New Clothes* and Father Given in *Faces Off*.

Beverley Longhurst
Ms Andrea Adelard / Female Newscaster / Prosecutor

Beverley graduated from Webber Douglas in 2000. Her theatre credits include *All My Sons* and *Rememberance of Things Past* for the Royal National Theatre and *Way Up Stream* at the Derby Playhouse. Television and film credits include *Armadillo, Man and Boy, Come Together* and *Jeffrey Archer - The Truth*.

Kristin Milward
Dr Desdemona Jones

Kristin trained at RADA. Theatre credits include seasons at The Crucible (Sheffield), The Library Theatre (Manchester) and The Phoenix (Leicester). Work in London includes *Plenty and Plunder* (Royal National Theatre), *Les Liasons Dangereuses* (RSC and on Broadway), *Snow Palace* (Tricycle Theatre), *Women of Troy* (The Orange Tree), *Devour the Snow* (The Bush), *The Bitter Tears of Petra Von Kant* (The Latchmere), *Uncle Vanya* and *Wounds to the Face* (The Wrestling School). Kristin has been seen on television in *Eastenders* and film credits include *The Fool, Scene of the Crime, The Lighthouse* and *City of the Dead*.

Trevor Thomas
Sir Huntley Palmer Jones

Theatre credits include *Krindlekrax, Of Mice and Men* (Nottingham Playhouse), *Boys Next Door* (Grace Theatre), *A Midsummer Night's Dream, The Passion* (National Theatre), *Pecong* (Tricycle Theatre), *Rum & Coca Cola, Play Mas* (Royal Court), *Whose Life is it Anyway* (Savoy and Mermaid) and *The Infernal Machine* (Lyric Hammersmith). Television Credits include *Silent Witness, Metropolis, Road Runner, Hold in Babylon, Murder at the Wedding, Minder, Strangers, The Professionals, Return of the Saint, No Problem, Give us a Break, Grange Hill, Truckers, Minder, A Dark Horse, The Torch, Us Girls, Back Up, Eastenders, Dangerfield, Melissa, London Bridge, McCallum* and *Murder of Stephen Lawrence*. Films include *Nine Lives of Thomas Katz, Black Joy, Stretch Hunter, Los Adolescentos, Inseminoid, International Velvet, Sheena Queen of the Jungle, Underworld* and *Gold Crew*. Trevor has also recently worked with Bob Hoskins on the British Telecom commercials.

Tariq Ali
Writer

Tariq Ali is a writer and filmmaker. He has written over a dozen books on world history and politics, five novels, and scripts for both stage and screen. The first novel of his *Islam Quintet, Shadows of the Pomegranate Tree*, was awarded the Archbishop San Clemente del Instituto Rosalia de Castro Prize for Best Foreign Language Fiction published in Spain in 1994 and, like the *Book of Saladin*, has been translated into several languages. His latest book is the critically *acclaimed The Clash of Fundamentalisms: Crusades, Jihads and Modernity* which was recently published in paperback by Verso. He is currently writing *Bush in Babylon: Recolonising Iraq* which Verso will publish in September 2003. Tariq Ali is an editor of New Left Review and lives in London.

Iqbal Khan
Director

Iqbal Khan is a director and actor. His numerous acting credits include Sir Robert Chiltern in *An Ideal Husband* (Leicester Haymarket Theatre), *Exit The King* (Edinburgh and Paris), *Hamlet, Uncle Vanya* and *The Homecoming* (The Edinburgh Fringe), *Huis Clos* (The Bloomsbury Theatre), and Tartuffe (The Bloomsbury Theatre) amongst others. While directing credits include *Beautiful Thing* (Oldham Coliseum), *Into The Woods* (Birmingham Hippodrome), *The Maids* (Old Red Lion) – Time Out's Critics Choice and *The Importance of Being Earnest* (The Union Theatre). Iqbal recently adapted, directed and played the lead role in *Othello* at Leicester Haymarket Theatre in November 2002, and is currently directing *Madam Butterfly* for Beaufort Opera at The Lyric Theatre, Hammersmith.

Kate Unwin Designer

Kate trained at De Montfort University, Leicester and works as Production Assistant at Leicester Haymarket Theatre as well as a freelance set and costume designer. Design credits include *An Ideal Husband* and *The Cripple of Inishmaan* (Leicester Haymarket Theatre), *Oedipus The King* (Leicester Adult Education), *Made In India* (Hangama Productions). Design Co-ordinator for *Sugar and Slugs* and *Othello* (directed by Iqbal Khan) all for the Leicester Haymarket Studio Theatre. Kate was also Assistant Designer for *The Threepenny Opera* (Haymarket Youth Theatre) on the Haymarket Theatre's Main Stage. Other credits include *Nanna's Nightingale* and *Stand* (Northampton Royal Theatre) both TIE shows; *The King of Spin* (Leicester Haymarket Theatre) for Bosworth Battlefield and *It's True What They Say About Cheese* at Phoenix Arts Centre, Leicester. Kate also created designs for the Haymarket Theatre's foyer space during Leicester Comedy Festival 2003 and the *Love In The 21st Century* project. She recently worked on *Bed* for the Haymarket Studio Theatre.

Miriam Spencer Lighting Designer

Miriam trained at the Royal Welsh College of Music & Drama and since graduating in 2000 has worked predominately in Bristol, Edinburgh and London on a range of theatre scales before happily settling at the Leicester Haymarket Theatre. Design work includes: *Miss Julie* (Tour of Hungary), Theatre Design Exhibition (Cardiff Visual Arts Centre), Three productions with Panpsychist Physical Theatre Company *C.O.D, Stigma, Illusions* (The Place London and Edinburgh Fringe) Rubicon Dance, *Boeing Boeing* (Cardiff), Arts Forum Launch (Gloucestershire County Council), *'cu2mrw.com'* (Leicester Haymarket Youth Theatre) and all re-lights for national tour of *Rose Blanche* for Box Clever Theatre company. Miriam was also Technical Manager for: Shakespeare @ The Tobacco Factory, Show of Strength Theatre Company, Partisan Theatre Company (Bristol), *'One'* (Compound Productions).

Ben Harrison Sound Designer

Ben started his career at the Liverpool Playhouse where design credits include, *The Cabinet of Dr Caligari* and *Dracula*. Since leaving Liverpool Ben's production credits have included *Blood Brothers* (UK Tour & West End), *Joseph and the Amazing Technicolor Dreamcoat* (UK Tour & West End), *Boogie Nights* (UK Tour), *Thank You For The Music* (UK Tour), *Rent* (UK Tour & West End), *The Pirates of Penzance* (UK Tour). Ben's recent design credits include *Blood Brothers* (UK Tour), *Whistle Down The Wind* (UK Tour), *The Roy Orbison Story* (UK Tour), *The Boy Friend* (UK Tour), *West Side Story* (Leicester Haymarket), *Richard Swerrun in Concert* (UK Tour) and the *Centenary Celebrations* at the Gaiety Theatre in Douglas.

Theatre Writing Partnership

Theatre Writing Partnership supports the development of new playwrights and new commissions across the theatres of the East Midlands.

This season's new productions of Tariq Ali's *The Illustrious Corpse* and Amanda Whittington's *Bollywood Jane* at Leicester Haymarket Theatre, Andy Barrett's *The Day That Kevin Came*, at Nottingham Playhouse and Hoipolloi's *The Man Next Door* at Royal and Derngate Theatres Northampton are fine examples of the producing theatre's huge commitment to new work.

If you are interested in playwriting and would like to learn more about opportunities to engage locally in workshops and competitions – or if you would simply like some feedback on a script – phone Esther Richardson or Sarah Françoise on 0115 947 4361, or email twp@nottinghamplayhouse.co.uk

Theatre Writing Partnership is funded jointly by: Leicester Haymarket Theatre; Derby Playhouse; New Perspectives; Northampton Theatres and Nottingham Playhouse.

THE
illuSTRiouS
CORPSE

First published in 2003 by Oberon Books Ltd.
(incorporating Absolute Classics)
521 Caledonian Road, London N7 9RH
Tel: 020 7607 3637 / Fax: 020 7607 3629

e-mail: oberon.books@btinternet.com
www.oberonbooks.com

A catalogue record for this book is available from the British
Library.

ISBN: 1 84002 382 1

Cover image: Robert Day © copyright Leicester Haymarket
Theatre.

Printed in Great Britain by Antony Rowe Ltd, Chippenham.

Characters

SIR HUNTLEY PALMER JONES
a Home Secretary

DR DESDEMONA JONES
his wife

SIR RICHARD EVERALL
Metropolitan Commissioner, Scotland Yard

MS ANDREA ADELARD
a special adviser

PROSECUTOR

FEMALE NEWSCASTER

Time: the present

Prologue

Screens light up. Year: 1979. A choreographed flashback with video footage of anti-apartheid rally. Music. South African freedom song.

DESDEMONA and HUNTLEY both in the video and in front of it on the stage.

VOICE-OVER: He was so black, so beautiful, so brave. That's why I fell in love with him.

HUNTLEY: (*In flashback.*) Brothers and sisters, comrades. I bring fraternal greetings to this picket from the Labour Party.

Boos, etc.

Like it or not our Party is committed to the anti-apartheid struggle. If it wasn't I wouldn't be a member. Nelson Mandela is our leader, too and we will struggle together against apartheid and the capitalism that sustains and arms it against the majority of the people. To our South African comrades I say: However desperate the situation, do not despair. However fearful the horrors they inflict on you, be unafraid. They think they can never lose because wealth is on their side. We, the people, need resources of a different kind. Audacity. Audacity. Audacity. We will take the enemy by surprise…

Loud applause, chants of 'Free Mandela', etc.

DESDEMONA: (*Voice-over/choreography.*) Then he saw me standing, noticed my admiring eyes, pretended not to look at my tits. It was a murky London day. Dark clouds. Drizzle. Misery. He laughed. His white teeth lit the sky.

HUNTLEY: (*Smiles.*) And to Margaret Thatcher and her gang who denounce Nelson Mandela as a terrorist, I have this to say: if Nelson Mandela is a terrorist, then I am a terrorist; if the ANC is terrorist, then I will donate money to it. Every leader of a national liberation struggle is denounced as a terrorist: Mandela, Che, Ho Chi Minh, Kenyatta, Arafat… So be it. We are with them.

Loud applause.

We are accused of terrorism when we speak of ruined homelands, nations without a name or an address. We are accused of terrorism when we speak of the cruelty and callousness of those who govern us by force. So be it. We will accept the name because in the end we will win. We are many they are few.

Applause, chants, songs, screens show Mandela, Masekala's trumpet blast, etc.

What's your name, lady?

DESDEMONA: Desdemona. Desdemona Williams. My mum works in the theatre at Clwd.

HUNTLEY: And I'm Huntley.

DESDEMONA: I know.

HUNTLEY: (*Bowing.*) Huntley Palmer Jones from Notting Hill. My old man worked in a biscuit factory all his life. In a town called Reading. He could have named me CLR Jones. Garfield Sobers Jones. Aneuran Bevan Jones, but…

DESDEMONA: He must have really loved biscuits. What do you like being called? Huntley or Hunter?

HUNTLEY: You may call me Othello.

DESDEMONA: Oh, may I? Thank you kindly, sir.

HUNTLEY: What do you do?

DESDEMONA: I'm a doctor, a GP. Two years.

HUNTLEY: Make yourself ready, Dr Desdemona Jones. Tonight you will lose your innocence.

DESDEMONA: And who will steal it?

HUNTLEY: (*Flexing muscles.*) Othello.

DESDEMONA: It was stolen many years ago, Othello. Another man, another country, another time.

HUNTLEY: All forgotten, I hope.

DESDEMONA: Yes, but there is something universal about all men despite differences of race or creed or politics or…

HUNTLEY: Good lady doctor. I promise you that I will be different from all the other lovers.

DESDEMONA: Really? How?

HUNTLEY: Where they gave you clouds I will give you rain. Where they gave you a ship, I'll give you the whole journey. Where they offer you an olive branch I'll present you with the whole tree.

DESDEMONA: Your modesty appeals to me.

They laugh, embrace and dance. They kiss.

End of choreographed flashback.

Screen: April 2003. DESDEMONA is alone in bed in her nightgown switching TV channels. Images of war in Iraq. Bush and Blair. Demonstrations. BBC World, CNN and al-Jazeera showing civilian casualties, children chanting: 'Who let the bombs out? Bush, Bush and Blair'; suddenly it's HUNTLEY in ministerial mode.

INTERVIEWER: Sir Huntley, three weeks ago you said on this programme that the Prime Minister was reckless and too close to Washington. You said and I quote, 'If we go

to war without UN support, I would find my position untenable.' Yet here you are still the Home Secretary.

HUNTLEY: It was I who was being reckless. I allowed emotion to override reason. I have already apologised to the Prime Minister and His Excellency the US Ambassador. In times of war, you know, I must support my leader.

INTERVIEWER: What would you say to your supporters who are implying that you were bought off…promised a better job after the reshuffle.

HUNTLEY: Nonsense. I am happy where I am. You know something. I have promises to keep before I sleep.

DESDEMONA: (*Aside.*) So do I…

Scene 1

Early morning. The living room in the Home Secretary's official residence in London. The lights reveal the Home Secretary, SIR HUNTLEY PALMER JONES, lying on the sofa, a half-finished tumbler of whisky by his side. He is dead. His wife, DESDEMONA, enters the room. She's wearing an old, flowery silk dressing-gown. She walks to the window and draws the curtains. Sunlight floods the room. Birds singing. She looks out of the window.

DESDEMONA: The azaleas are early this year.

She hums. Giant azalea appears on screen.

I said the azaleas are already in flower and its only early April. Considered coldly and clinically, one has to admit that something's gone badly wrong. Somewhere. Everywhere. When we were young we used to struggle for the restoration of nature, for public parks, public beaches, public spaces. You know, the nuts and bolts of everyday life. Tranquillity. Beauty. Freedom. Social justice. Socialism meant the fulfilment of all these needs.

And now? Everything fragmented. Everything polluted. Not just the environment. Politics, business, culture. Even our aesthetic needs have to be repressed. And on top of everything else we now have a war every year. (*Looking at the body.*) That's what your party's slogan should be. New Labour, New War. But the kids are out on the streets again and it's great to see and hear them. That's something the renegades told us could never happen again. World without conflict and all that shit. Yes, millions against the war, but we couldn't stop it. I wonder whether the flowers were early this year in Baghdad? How is the scent of the date-palm affected by a daisy-cutter? Othello! Did you hear me? Why don't you reply? Othello? Haven't called him that since the last century. (*Aside.*) Oh my God. I forgot. Last night. He's dead. He really is dead and I forgot. It happened last night. At first he was very alive. Then he was very dead. I was very tired. So, I just went to bed. I'd come back exhausted after a bad day at the hospital. He shouldn't have picked a fight with me. He really shouldn't have done that. (*Walks to the body.*) I can see his obituary now. Sir Huntley Palmer Jones. A man of lightning reflexes and snappy judgements. (*Shudders.*) That's not why they made him Home Secretary. Its because he agreed to become a white sheep. That's how he became the first black politician to get a senior Cabinet post. And now he's dead. Just like a big, black fly caught in a spider's web. I used to love him so much. Did I really love all of him? No, that's an exaggeration. Not all of him. How can one love someone else's liver, intestines, arteries or oesophagus. Oh well. He's gone now. (*She paces up and down silently for a few moments.*) To deal with this mess now or after breakfast. That is the question. The exquisite aroma of freshly-ground coffee? Organic, from Papua, New Guinea. Fair Trade stamp. Excellent quality. But it will have to wait. I should ring the police. No. First, Ophelia. (*Aside.*) We named our daughter Ophelia.

She never forgave us. She hated him. Had her hair cropped, and ran off to Sydney. In Australia. She came out. I met Judith. They were happy, but the future Home Secretary was miserable. I suppose he was thinking of a grand wedding with the Prime Minister present… He kept arguing with her as if she had committed a crime. And my little Philly galloped off to a far away continent. He's a creep mum. Why don't you dump him and come with me. You're a doctor. You'll never be out of work. Leave this place. Its dead. Everything's rotten, especially my dad. That's what she said. Nothing airy-fairy about our Ophelia. She'll be really upset now that he's gone. She would have been marching with the kids. She would have burnt her dad's effigy. (*Goes to the phone, dials.*) Hullo, Philly, is that you Philly? Well, no. Of course I knew it was you. How's Judith. Oh, good. Good! I've got bad news. Is it bad news? It must be. It must be. Your father's dead. (*Longish pause.*) Ophelia! I'm shocked. I really am. He's dead, so please… I need you here for the funeral. What do you mean you'll think about it? And could you stop eating while we speak. I don't care if the mushroom and pumpkin soup is delicious. Your father's dead. Will you ring me after you've finished your soup. Dear God. (*Re-dials 999.*) Come on, come on. Have they privatised this, too? Yes, hullo. Police. (*Another pause.*) This is Dr Desdemona Jones. I wish to report a sudden death. Sir Huntley Palmer Jones. Yes that's what I said. Wrong. He was the Home Secretary. He's now dead. He might have been murdered. Yes murdered.

She barely puts the phone down when there's a noise of a car screeching to a halt, car doors slamming and front doorbell ringing. DESDEMONA leaves the room.

Noises backstage.

She returns with a very pretty young woman, power-dressed.

The two women bristle with hostility.

ANDREA: (*Visibly upset on seeing the body, but manages to control herself.*) I can't believe it. He really is dead. For a moment, I thought it might be one of your horrible jokes.

DESDEMONA: You're green beneath your rouge, dear. If you want to go and be sick that's fine by me. I think you know where the bathroom is… How in hell's name did you get here? Well? I ring 999 and get a Special Adviser from the Home Office. Just like a fuckogram.

ANDREA: Please, Dr Jones. I'm not…

DESDEMONA: And what do you know about my horrible jokes. Did you offer special advice on those as well? (*Pauses to look at the other woman's expression.*) Oh that joke. What did you expect me to do.

As she talks we see it happening on the screen.

I switch on his computer and there's an intriguing addition on the toolbar. Could that be right? Toolbar? So I press the mouse, new images. A lovely naked Special Adviser occupies the screen. There you were, my dear, displaying all your goods. Front and back, just in case he was in two minds. Your breasts surprised me. They were like hunting horns. Never knew he went in for that. What possessed the idiot to add you to his toolbar?

ANDREA: (*Faintly.*) I don't know. My stupid fault…

DESDEMONA: Was it really horrible of me to get the image printed and send it off as a New Year card to all our friends?

New Year card on screen.

Did that upset you? I'm sorry. Forgive me. I was a bit overwrought at the time. (*Bursts out laughing.*) But it was very funny. I'm told you were the toast of more than one party that year. You shouldn't have too many problems getting a new job. Ever thought about hostessing a game-show on Newsnight? They could call it New Labour's Toolbar. Just one word of advice. Change the power haircut below your waist. Get a merkin.

ANDREA: A merkin..?

DESDEMONA: Yes.

ANDREA: What is it?

DESDEMONA: A pubic wig. Very popular with New Labour. The Prime Minister wears one on his head…

ANDREA: Please…

DESDEMONA: (*Angry.*) How the hell did you get here? Can't be telepathy. He's dead. How dare you disrupt my privacy. Can't even grieve in peace.

ANDREA: I was already on my way here with some of his papers. Files he had to read today on the way to work. Then Special Branch rang.

DESDEMONA: With some of his papers, really. Couldn't they wait? Or were you planning a quickie before you left for work? He told me you sometimes did. Oh, yes, once I knew, he was only too keen to confess, the way men do. No self-control. I would have known anyway. Huntley could never deny his underlings innocent pleasures. The cleaning woman used to complain of stains on the leather. Did you…on his desk? Why? Was the settee uncomfortable?

ANDREA: I didn't want to, but it turned him on. He said that you… I'm sorry. I'm not going to discuss anything like that with you. I mean he's lying there. Dead and…

DESDEMONA: Of course not. You don't want to hurt me. Sisterly solidarity much appreciated Ms Adelard. Thank you.

ANDREA: You did say murder, didn't you?

DESDEMONA: I did?

ANDREA: Well, that's what the police reported.

DESDEMONA: They did?

ANDREA: I thought we should have a word first. You know, just in case there are things that might be damaging if revealed to the police and…

DESDEMONA: Don't worry sweetie. You're safe. It had nothing to do with you. So pack up your tits, adjust your briefs and ask for a transfer.

ANDREA: I have to do my job. Surely you can see that…

DESDEMONA: I surely can, though we might disagree on the job description. Listen. I think I'd rather talk to the police directly. Why aren't they here? Have you informed Downing Street? Damage limitation organised?

ANDREA: Yes, yes but the Prime Minister still hasn't been informed. He's just returned from the war summit in Texas. Iran's next on the list you know. We're saving Syria for later. They didn't want to wake him up. I know you lot think he's just a poodle…

DESDEMONA: Poodle? Poodle? Oh no. More a mastiff, snarling at the leash. The scent of blood turns him on. After all it's much more exciting than sorting out health or education or transport. I can just see him in Texas. First a little joint prayer to Jesus. Then the mask of piety to conceal the delight as he receives new orders. Let's go and bomb Tehran. Yeah, sure, Mr President. Its got to be done. You know Prime Minister, I'd love to bomb Beijing one day. After all they really have weapons of mass destruction. Sure Mr President that would be great, but mightn't they use them? Shouldn't we sort out Iran first? They might cave in if we just park our aircraft carriers in the straits of Hormuz. What about a new road map.

ANDREA: Slightly unfair. Anyway it's a bit early to wake the Prime Minister up…

DESDEMONA: I'm sure he'll be relieved. He never really trusted Othello.

ANDREA: Othello?

DESDEMONA: I called him that when we first met. Then it became darling, then Huntley and, more recently Hunt. You know. You stupid Hunt… And what did you call him, let me guess. It must have been something obvious…

ANDREA: (*Aside.*) Unlike Othello.

DESDEMONA: Biscuit. That's what you called him. Let me nibble you, my little biscuit. Did he ever get stale?

ANDREA: (*Aside.*) How does she know? If she's right that Biscuit never enjoyed real trust where will they relocate me? (*To DESDEMONA.*) Why do you think the Prime Minister never trusted him?

DESDEMONA: Don't blame him for that. He knew that Sir Huntley's basic loyalty was to his own career. It's a New Labour disease. When your biscuit thought the war might go wrong he distanced himself, didn't he? They hate that sort of talk in Downing Street. So I think secretly they'll all be relieved. Someone else can be bought off with the job. Time old Mandelson was brought in again. As Home Secretary he could tap Gordon Brown's phone. Have you talked to the Deputy Prime Minister?

ANDREA: Yes, yes, of course. Alastair will be calling you directly. Please don't worry. Everything's under control.

DESDEMONA: What's under control? You don't even know what happened.

ANDREA: It's when we don't know what really happened that control becomes vital.

DESDEMONA: (*Laughs loudly.*) How very stupid.

ANDREA: Otherwise there's a frenzy of speculation. Wild speculation. Dozens of different versions in the press. So we must have a single narrative. One story. The same beginning, middle and end. That's control.

DESDEMONA: And the truth?

ANDREA: The truth? (*Into dictaphone.*) Note to self… Ring Harvey Nics for merkin… Biscuit obit… Note to imbedded journalists: Sir Huntley Palmer Jones was a man of lightning reflexes and snappy judgements and a close personal friend of the prime minister.

Doorbell.

As DESDEMONA leaves the room, ANDREA, wiping a tear, rushes to the corpse, kisses its lips and puts its right hand on her breast.

Poor Biscuit. What happened to you? Why did you die, Biscuit and leave your poor Nibbles on her own. Talk to me. Nibble me. She insulted my tits. You loved them didn't you? Oh Biscuit…

DESDEMONA: (*Offstage.*) Come in, Sir Richard. I was hoping it would be you.

SIR RICHARD: (*Enters.*) Well it's not every day that a Home Secretary drops dead. The photographs won't take long. Thought I'd take them myself, just to avoid…well you know.

DESDEMONA: (*Whispers.*) Fine. There's a very stupid woman in there. Special Adviser? You know. Andrea

Adelard. Could you get rid of her? She was loyal to him alright. Loyal as a dog…

ANDREA: (*Recovering her composure. Aside.*) Bitch. Good morning Sir Richard.

SIR RICHARD: Good morning to you Miss Adelard. (*Soft voice.*) I think, if you don't mind, I had better speak to Lady, oops…sorry, Dr Jones, on her own. I'm sure we'll be in touch later. You understand?

ANDREA: Only too well. We'll be in touch very soon. Well goodbye Sir Richard. Goodbye Lady Jones.

Exit ANDREA.

SIR RICHARD begins to take pics of the body from every possible angle with a tiny camera.

DESDEMONA: Didn't know you had such a small one. The camera.

SIR RICHARD: The latest. It's all digitalised now and these photographs are already being transmitted to the central computer at the Yard.

DESDEMONA: How reassuring. Would you like some coffee Sir Richard?

SIR RICHARD: Somehow it seems wrong to be drinking coffee with such an illustrious corpse still in the room.

DESDEMONA: Why? It might appear odd if I was offering you scrambled eggs on toast with a slither of smoked salmon, but coffee?

SIR RICHARD: Oh well. Perhaps a bit later.

DESDEMONA: Scrambled eggs on wild smoked salmon?

SIR RICHARD: No, no. Coffee. Now Dr Jones, please sit down. Thank you. Now just tell me, in your own time, exactly what happened. Try and remember every detail.

It could be important. One more thing. I do have to warn you that anything you say could be…

DESDEMONA: Used in evidence against me?

SIR RICHARD: Exactly.

DESDEMONA: I was so hoping you'd say that…I love it when they say that in murder movies. That's what I want. I want the evidence used against me. Do you remember 'Witness for the Prosecution' with Charles Laughton and Marlene Dietrich?

SIR RICHARD: A bit before my time, I'm afraid. But this is real, Dr Jones. You do realise that? This is not television, though I dare say, given the position of the corpse, it might become a movie one day.

DESDEMONA: (*Looking anxiously at the body.*) Why? Is the position of the corpse unusual?

SIR RICHARD: He was the Home Secretary.

DESDEMONA: (*Laughs.*) Oh I see. What do you mean when you say it's not television? I think it is exactly that. I mean everything we see these days is real and unreal. Politics, sex, football, television, even theatre. It may be wishful thinking, but how many people out there have convinced themselves that the Home Secretary really has been bumped off. Don't you agree? Surely you must. I mean all those police shows we see…

SIR RICHARD: Those, dear lady, are definitely unreal. We all appreciate the free PR, but the lads laugh themselves stupid. Back to basics, Dr Jones. You've just repeated that you think the Home Secretary was bumped off. Obviously there'll be an inquest, but I can't see any signs of violence myself. He looks so peaceful.

DESDEMONA: Yes, yes. It looks as if he died in his sleep. Not really. He was murdered.

SIR RICHARD: (*Humouring her.*) How do you know?

DESDEMONA: I was here.

SIR RICHARD: Okay, then. Tell me. Who murdered him?

DESDEMONA: I did.

SIR RICHARD: (*Clearly agitated. Switches off tape-recorder.*) I know you're upset Dr Jones, but please…you're incriminating yourself. I suppose I better seal off the area where the crime was committed.

He opens his case and unpacks a little fence and masking tape, rushes to the sofa, put the fence around it and masking tape on floor. He looks pleased with himself even though he's out of breath.

DESDEMONA: (*Smiles.*) I think the exercise did you some good.

SIR RICHARD: Haven't done that since I was a sergeant. Please don't cross the forbidden zone. I don't want any interference with the finger or foot prints.

DESDEMONA: They'll all be mine anyway. I can't see why you're making such a fuss. What's the problem. I've confessed. You don't need any proof.

SIR RICHARD: Dr Jones, please come to your senses. I can understand you might have been fed up with him. I've read the Intelligence briefings on your relationship. I also know you're still a bit of a subversive.

DESDEMONA: Really? An old Labour lag like myself? How on earth did you deduce that?

SIR RICHARD: You subscribe to the London Review of Books don't you? You see we knew that. And you were on the big antiwar demonstration.

DESDEMONA: There were over a million other people there. Othello should have been there too.

SIR RICHARD: Now please Dr Jones, I know you're angry and upset, but…

DESDEMONA: I'm in full possession, Sir Richard. Isn't that the phrase. Full possession of mental faculties. Well, I am. I'm a senior consultant at the Royal Free. I operated on three patients yesterday. And successfully. Could easily do the same today. You don't have a problem, do you? A touch of the prostate, perhaps?

SIR RICHARD: No, no, no. I'm fine.

DESDEMONA: Are you sure. You're nearly sixty aren't you?

SIR RICHARD: Well since you mention it, I…I do suffer a bit from hesitancy. The flow is variable. Takes longer than it should sometimes.

DESDEMONA: I could recommend a very good urologist. I assume you're insured.

SIR RICHARD: Well, er er I am. Just to avoid the queues.

DESDEMONA: Of course. I wonder what your PSA reading is?

SIR RICHARD: PSA?

Screen lights up with Prostate Specific Antigen and figures of prostate cancer.

DESDEMONA: Oh Prostate Specific Antigen. Thank God women don't have prostates. Look. If yours is over 4.2 a prostate cancer screening might be beneficial.

SIR RICHARD: (*Shaken.*) Cancer! Look all I said was that I don't wee as well as I did and you start talking cancer… (*Recovering.*) Sorry, I got distracted. Dr Jones, I must ask you to think very carefully before you say anything else concerning your husband.

DESDEMONA: Please believe me Sir Richard. Yesterday, I despatched your Home Secretary gently into the night. (*Laughs.*) Don't you think you should call an ambulance. He's beginning to… (*Sniffs.*) you know.

 SIR RICHARD: You hated him. Didn't you?

 DESDEMONA: Of course not. I loved him greatly and then it stopped. Funny seeing him dead like that.

 SIR RICHARD: Funny ha-ha or funny peculiar?

 DESDEMONA: Both! This morning when I saw him lying there, I felt compassion, even tenderness. Don't get the wrong idea. Its only because he's dead.

 SIR RICHARD: You're in a state of complete shock, Dr Jones…

 DESDEMONA: No, but you clearly are. A steaming cup of coffee to calm your nerves?

 SIR RICHARD: (*Stealing a glance at the corpse.*) A latte would be lovely.

 DESDEMONA: (*Sweetly.*) Afraid I've only got Nescafe. Will that do? Good. (*Exits.*)

SIR RICHARD: (*Agitated. Dials on his mobile.*) Hullo. Jonathan? Richard Everall here. The news is not good. I'll organise an autopsy immediately, but she continues to insist he was murdered. She did. I'm not joking. No, she's no more insane than you or I. In fact considerably less. No, no, no. She's totally calm and self-contained. Dare I say it, she's relaxed and even relieved. Calm down, please. I know what's expected and I will try, but if she insists…of course I understand. I've yet to debrief her. Give me a few hours. No, Jonathan. The Prime Minister having a word with her is a bad and provocative idea. Oh I know. By the way the Hitler Youth was here when I arrived…and I…she's with you?

Oh good. Keep here there. No phone calls to stray lovers in the media. One leak and we're done for. I think we can keep it quiet for a few hours, but once the news is out the hacks will be swarming all over the street. In her present state, Lady Jones will tell them what she told me. Well, I'll leave that one with you. My advice is not to send Miss Adelard here on any mission... Fine.

DESDEMONA returns with two mugs and a sugar bowl. Coffee is served.

DESDEMONA: Sugar?

SIR RICHARD: No thanks.

DESDEMONA: Doesn't affect the prostate, you know.

SIR RICHARD: (*Stern.*) Dr Jones, why would you want to murder the Home Secretary?

DESDEMONA: Murder sounds wrong. Should we say execution?

SIR RICHARD: You may say what you like. I have to treat this as a murder enquiry.

DESDEMONA: Fine. Murder, eh? I suppose the word is useful. After all, he murdered his past and became part of a government that's murdering the present and, by extension, the future. So I executed him. Had to do something. You could call it a pre-emptive strike, to encourage regime-change. You feel that someone is going to do something terrible and you take them out before they can. Couldn't just sit and watch Huntley and his chums murder everything I valued. Perhaps it was a bit excessive? What do you think? Overkill?

SIR RICHARD: I'm not quite sure I understand you.

DESDEMONA: You wouldn't.

SIR RICHARD: Try me.

DESDEMONA: No thanks.

SIR RICHARD: Dr Jones, are you seriously trying to tell me that you committed a murder because of some philosophical differences?

DESDEMONA: Far too lofty, Sir Richard. Implies they have a philosophy, apart from staying in power and lining their pockets. Our differences were political. We've been quarrelling for the last seven years, ever since the day he was flattered into accepting a knighthood.

Screen: HUNTLEY on knees being knighted by Queen.

Made me sick.

SIR RICHARD: I can understand the need. He was a self-made man. He achieved wealth and power and…

DESDEMONA: You too have an honour. I know. But then I'm not married to you. From my experience all self-made people these days…men and women…have been made by other people who themselves were made by a combination of circumstances, history and sordid deals. Sir Huntley Palmer Jones was well aware of this fact. He knew that the time-servers who gave him a leg-up were men without substance. In a totally honest society where men and women depended on their own merits and abilities, the bulk of our politicians would have been on the threshold of power as door-keepers. The more imaginative types would have served time in prison. Instead of which –

SIR RICHARD: They are respectable leaders of our country I know.

DESDEMONA: Respectable? Politics is a way of making money now. You help the less rich get more rich and when you retire as a Minister they give you a job. Or you do privatisation deals and end up with stock options and Directorships. It's the same everywhere. In Brazil or Bolivia or Peru the peasants are fighting back. Here the peasants have become serfs.

SIR RICHARD: (*Aside.*) She really is quite nutty. She probably did kill him. (*To DESDEMONA.*) But why kill him now? Last night. Was there something specific that triggered your anger?

DESDEMONA: The initial accumulation of resentments is always primitive, but then they begin to grow. They reach a new stage. A new level of maturity. They become multi-layered. And then, one day, something happens which a few years ago would only have angered me. Yesterday when he went back on his pledge I decided to despatch him.

SIR RICHARD: I always thought someone like you would always prefer to be the victim. Never the executioner.

DESDEMONA: How philosophical of you and how sweet. But please don't judge me by my appearance. I may look like a bleeding-heart liberal, but there is iron in my soul. Do you want to hear it all?

SIR RICHARD: That's why I'm here.

DESDEMONA: It's a long story.

SIR RICHARD: I have all the time in the world.

DESDEMONA: No you don't. The vultures will start circling very soon..

The phone rings.

She crosses the room to pick it up.

DESDEMONA: Oh, hullo. Didn't think you'd ring back. (*To SIR RICHARD.*) It's my daughter from Australia. I'm not sure. Probably in a week or so. You'll come. Oh Philly

31

that's wonderful. I better go now because the Metropolitan Chief Commissioner of Scotland Yard is here. We're discussing your father's death. Didn't I tell you? I am sorry. I did. It was me. I'm serious,. Philly? She put the phone down on me. I always knew she was fond of him.

SIR RICHARD: Dr Jones, do you really think you could convince a jury to acquit you? A good prosecutor would destroy you. Thought about that?

DESDEMONA: I think of little else.

PROSECUTOR in.

 PROSECUTOR: Why did you kill your husband?

DESDEMONA: His enormous vanity led him to betray all his principles. He became a complete time-server. A mouthpiece for the worst elements in our society. His narcissism made him an insufferable bore.

PROSECUTOR: With respect Dr Jones, if your criteria were to be more generally deployed, no Government minister would ever be safe. I'm sure History will treat him much more kindly.

DESDEMONA: If he's remembered at all, it will be solely because of what I did. I've made him a quiz show question. Which Home Secretary was murdered while still in office, by whom and in what year? Anyone? Four buzzers will simultaneously explode. Four voices will shout in unison: ' Sir Huntley Palmer Jones by his wife Desdemona in 2003.'

SIR RICHARD: We better do this properly now.

SIR RICHARD / PROSECUTOR: Where did you and your future husband first meet?

DESDEMONA: It was over twenty years ago…

As she stands up and paces the stage, darkness and spotlights.

We were picketing the South African Embassy.

SIR RICHARD: Love at first sight?

DESDEMONA: Lust at first sight. Love came later.

PROSECUTOR: What was it that attracted you…

DESDEMONA: His politics and his body. In that order.

SIR RICHARD: You can't be in love with a chap because of his politics…can you?

DESDEMONA: Not now. Not in the Labour Party. In those days you could.

Screen shows Tony Benn in full flow at Labour Party conference.

PROSECUTOR: So, it was spiritual?

DESDEMONA: Political and physical. Not spiritual.

SIR RICHARD: But it was politics that really turned you on… Forgive me. I'm just trying to understand the nature of your relationship.

DESDEMONA: Let me explain. In those days, listening to him gave me a mental orgasm. (*Touches her head.*) Here. At first I thought that would suffice. Like going to a restaurant where the hors d'oeuvres is such a knockout that you think you can do without anything else. But you're wrong. Deep down you're famished, waiting desperately for the next course and…

SIR RICHARD: And what about the dessert? Isn't that vital. A last sweetening of the mouth. Turkish Delight. Sorry. I mean could you be a bit more specific?

DESDEMONA: About what?

SIR RICHARD: Well, er…er…what was it about him that you really liked. I mean physically.

DESDEMONA: I loved his body smells. His armpits were delicious. I can't stand English bodies. Impersonal and odourless.

Phone rings.

As she turns to answer it Sir RICHARD smells his armpits and smiles.

PROSECUTOR out.

Yes. This is her. Can't talk now. I'm in a meeting at the moment. Huntley's still asleep, I'm afraid. He was poorly last night. Ring later. Bye. My nephew. Desperate to be an intern at the Home Office. I promised his mother. Perhaps he could go to Scotland Yard. You could fit him up couldn't you.

SIR RICHARD: That's what we're really good at… I mean we might find him a placement, but please carry on…this is very important for solving this mystery.

DESDEMONA: Mystery? If you insist. Well sometimes I'd lift the sheets, turn him over on his stomach and give him a gentle spank. We both enjoyed that. I loved to feel his big, captive body against mine. Did you know he had pink testicles?

SIR RICHARD: No. This mustn't get out. It could seriously discredit the Government.

DESDEMONA: I'm amazed you gave him security clearance. I mean. Let's forget it. Should I carry on?

SIR RICHARD: Yes, yes please.

DESDEMONA: Sometimes we used to have a bath together and…

SIR RICHARD: (*As in a hypnotic trance.*) Really? (*And then very alert and blurts this out before he can control himself.*) How big was his column?

DESDEMONA: Is any of this really relevant to your investigation?

SIR RICHARD: (*Pleading.*) Yes, of course…please don't stop now.

DESDEMONA: Why is our sex-life so important?

SIR RICHARD: Well, er, just to understand what went wrong with the relationship to make you do what you did, if you really did. Did you?

DESDEMONA: Yes I did.

SIR RICHARD: Then carry on, please.

DESDEMONA: That was all a very long time ago, Sir Richard. Naughty man. Too much reality television, eh?

SIR RICHARD: (*Pompous.*) So, when did you first begin to feel a sense of alienation from your husband. Was it sudden or gradual?

DESDEMONA: Political or sexual alienation?

SIR RICHARD: (*Exasperated.*) BOTH!

DESDEMONA: Which should we discuss first?

SIR RICHARD: I suppose we should have sex first.

DESDEMONA: A bit difficult. It was simultaneous.

SIR RICHARD: I'm not sure I…

DESDEMONA: Both happened at the same time. He became politically impotent and I went off him.

SIR RICHARD: Er. I see. When exactly?

DESDEMONA: It was a few days after the election victory in 1997.

PROSECUTOR in.

PROSECUTOR: In other words from May 1997 till yesterday, you and Sir Huntley had ceased to have, er, sexual relations.

DESDEMONA: No.

SIR RICHARD: Oh?

DESDEMONA: Dear me, Sir Richard, you're almost as slow as W.

PROSECUTOR: Just answer my questions, Dr Jones.

DESDEMONA: He became politically impotent. That made me sexually indifferent.

SIR RICHARD: But you said…

DESDEMONA: I couldn't bear to touch him. This soft flesh became his prisoner. I let him do what he wanted. It was joyless sex. Do you know what I mean?

SIR RICHARD: Well, not exactly, but I do…

DESDEMONA: Why not rephrase your question: Dr Jones did you ever have an orgasm with your husband after he became a government minister? No, Sir Richard, I did not. (*Pause.*) I thought it might be possible to win him back. He might change. Last night I realised I was wrong.

PROSECUTOR: When did it start going wrong?

DESDEMONA: A day after the election victory. I'll never forget that night. I was with him at the count. When we got back home there was a large crowd of friends. Ours and Ophelia's. It was pure joy. Thatcherism had been wiped out. Or so we thought. Othello…I mean Huntley was singing songs: The Red Flag. The Internationale and of course 'He's the Man the very fat man that waters the worker's beer.'

SIR RICHARD: Don't think I know the words of any of them.

DESDEMONA: Nobody does now. (*Sings.*): 'The People's Flag is deepest blue. Its been dyed by you know who. And every loyal boardroom peer, is serving time once a year.'

SIR RICHARD: That's very clever. Who made that up.

DESDEMONA: Huntley. The day he became Home Secretary. Self-hatred fed the cynicism. But on that glorious night when the Tories virtually disappeared off our screens and became history, we were all drunk. Alcohol, but also joy. Huntley was in boastful mood. Education, health, welfare, railway privatisation, public transport. He would not give up till the Thatcherite counter-revolution had been rolled back all the way and if that shit Blair tried to stop them, the labour movement would sort him out. He'd been useful to win the election, but now…I suppose I was naive to take him so seriously.

SIR RICHARD: I remember that night too. A bit different where I was. The Daily Telegraph election-night party. They, too, thought Thatcherism was all over. Saw more than one venerable wiping away a tear. How wrong they were. (*Chuckles.*) How did matters proceed after that night?

DESDEMONA: Two days later and it was all over. Huntley came back from seeing the new leaders of our country. They'd offered him a pissy little job. Testing him out. You clean the lavatories for a while and then, after an inspection, we'll see if we can promote you. You know the sort of thing you might say to a former criminal applying to join the Special Branch…

SIR RICHARD: Afraid the traffic there is the other way round.

DESDEMONA: Yes, I see. Anyway Huntley had to cleanse himself of even the tiniest bit of socialism. It's the dental floss treatment. (*Gestures.*) He was only too happy to be a Junior Minister for the Environment. All he had to do was keep his mouth shut and indulge in some photo-opportunism. Pics with cows before they went mad, with whales before they were harpooned, a swim in a stream to show it wasn't polluted. It took six months to get rid of the fungus from his skin. And, no. He did not consult me before accepting the job. He'd been celebrating elsewhere.

Flashback scene.

Late night. Modest kitchen in Hackney. DESDEMONA is sitting at the table reading and making notes. Sound of key in door and HUNTLEY staggers in. She ignores him. He does a little jig.

DESDEMONA: Which bar was it?

HUNTLEY: No 10 Downing Street. You be careful woman, how you address me. You're speaking to a member of the Government.

DESDEMONA: You must be very drunk.

HUNTLEY: Why not. It's not every day that the Prime Minister offers you a job. I've accepted.

DESDEMONA: You what?

HUNTLEY: (*Putting on a West Indian accent.*) I wish my old man was alive. He'd be so thrilled. An immigrant from Tobago, who comes here with nothing. Works in a factory all his life. Dies with nothing in the bank. And his son is a member of de government. Oh man, he would have celebrated.

DESDEMONA: I'm not so sure. He might just have knocked you out. He was always going on about slavery. Do you remember the night he took us to hear CLR James. You were so proud. Eyes shining. Remember what the old man talked about that night. In order to keep slavery going, everyone, senator and banker, becomes a slave to Caesar. The threat of a Spartacus makes them all slaves to the system.

HUNTLEY: Spartacus, shmartacus. What you talking about woman. Why do you never celebrate with me. Is there any whisky in the house. Yes, there is. Don't you try and hide it from me. (*Searches for the whisky and finds it. Pours himself a large glass.*)

DESDEMONA: Why the hell did they want you?

HUNTLEY: They really need me. Yeah baby. They need me.

DESDEMONA: So that 'shit Blair' offered you a job?

HUNTLEY: Shh. This place might be bugged. They need an honest black face in their government. I'm the son of a worker. Not a petty-bourgeois hustler trying to rush up the ladder.

DESDEMONA: Give yourself a chance. Early days.

He carries on drinking.

Careful, Mr Jones. Your liver might conk out before you can roll back the Thatcher counter-revolution.

HUNTLEY: That look on your face. Wipe it off, baby. I'm your Othello. Nothing's changed.

DESDEMONA: You're going to be up to your eyes in shit. No need to spout it as well. Understand what you're doing.

HUNTLEY: Just because I'm black I have to be radical. Is that what you think?

DESDEMONA: No. There are lots of black and Asian opportunists on the make. Nothing to do with colour. It's politics. Intellect. Honesty. Principles. Remember.

HUNTLEY: Times have changed…

DESDEMONA: The motto of every time-server since time immemorial. Times have changed. Things are much worse than before. Does that mean we just cave in to the corporations. That's what these boys are about. Don't do it, Othello. Its not worth it…Othello.

Suddenly he begins to weep. The whisky has made him maudlin. As she moves towards him, he drops on the floor and begins to crawl on all fours.

DESDEMONA: Othello, Othello.

HUNTLEY: (*Sobbing.*) I've sold my soul, Des. I've sold my soul. I've made a pact with Satan. Leave me to rot. I'm not good enough for you. Its just that with the world changed so much I don't think there's another way any more. The flood carried me away. I can no longer judge or understand. I let myself drift. I'm tired of swimming against the stream. Stay with me. Without you I'd sink even more…

DESDEMONA: There's always another way, Othello. Always. Come on, get up. Let me get you to bed.

She tries to lift him. He grabs and brings her down and kisses her passionately on her lips. She pushes him away gently, gets up and pull him upright and pushes him out of the room.

End Flashback.

SIR RICHARD: That night when you took him to bed. Did you make love?

 DESDEMONA: He was in no fit state to make love.

SIR RICHARD: Oh really? I thought men like him…

DESDEMONA: Always had a hard-on? No, they don't. Black men have the same problems as anyone else.

 SIR RICHARD: But if he'd wanted to, you would have agreed? Dr Jones, please concentrate. This is a very important question.

DESDEMONA: (*Bewildered.*) My husband comes home dead drunk, crawls on the floor, tells me he's sold out on all his beliefs and all you want to know is whether I would have shagged him if he had been capable. What on earth is going on?

SIR RICHARD: It's everywhere you look Dr Jones. We live in a voyeuristic culture. The personal before the political. The economic before the personal. Sex. Money. Celebrity. Big Brother. Hello magazine. Dumbed down BBC. Bread, bullshit and sport. I hadn't realised that it had infected me. I'm not sure I object. Its made me much more human. You don't agree?

DESDEMONA: It's debased everything. Politics, culture, sport and, yes, sex as well.

PROSECUTOR: Do you always speak with the voice of the metropolitan liberal elite, Mrs Jones?

DESDEMONA: Is it elitist to challenge stupidity?

PROSECUTOR: Would you not agree, Lady Jones, that people have a democratic right to be stupid, to enjoy crap TV, to read The Sun, to do whatever they want?

DESDEMONA: But the elite promotes a culture that breeds ignorance. This top-down populism can turn our lovey-

feely apolitical citizens into crazed warmongers. One day they weep for a dead princess. The next day they cheer a European city being bombed.

SIR RICHARD: There you go again.

DESDEMONA: Perhaps you could explain why the sight of a Kosovan refugee leads to the bombing of Belgrade, but the plight of the Palestinian leaves our great humanitarian government totally cold.

SIR RICHARD: You've lost me there. I'm just not political.

DESDEMONA: Who decides? It's always the men at the top. All this fake, pseudo-populism is carefully orchestrated. Dyke, Murdoch? What's the difference.

SIR RICHARD: Oh there is a difference. The first is appointed by the Government. The second helps keep the Government in power. (*Pause.*) Would you have shagged him that night if he'd tried…

DESDEMONA: (*Stony.*) Shagged who?

SIR RICHARD: The late Home Secretary.

DESDEMONA: Is this an official question? I don't know.

PROSECUTOR: Dr Jones I will ask you something once again. Perhaps the repetition will reinvigorate your memory. You're one hundred per cent sure that your decision to terminate your husband's life was provoked by political disgust rather than sexual jealousy.

DESDEMONA: (*Slightly irritated.*) Well, obviously.

PROSECUTOR: Remarkable.

SIR RICHARD: Remarkable. In all my experience as a police officer, and I spent several years in the CID, I have never encountered a case of this nature. I just don't think a jury would believe you.

DESDEMONA: I think I might convince them. You just don't understand, do you? If it had been sexual jealousy I'd have left ages ago. Andrea wasn't the first, you know. (*Aside.*) Though she's definitely the last. And you Sir Richard, do you think your wife doesn't know you've been unfaithful.

 SIR RICHARD: (*Shifty.*) I don't understand.

 DESDEMONA: You seriously think she doesn't know you're playing rookie with that lovely young lassie on the beat.

 SIR RICHARD: (*Aside.*) Oh my God. How on earth do you…it's not true. Ugly rumours that's all.

 DESDEMONA: Well, well, well. Your wife does know. Don't doubt that for a moment. Doesn't really matter does it? That's all I'm trying to say. Do you wish to continue with your interrogation?

 PROSECUTOR: Could you describe your last encounter with Sir Huntley.

 DESDEMONA: Sexual or political?

 PROSECUTOR: Lady Jones, let's stick to the facts. What exactly happened last night?

DESDEMONA: You're fast-forwarding too quickly. Don't you want an account of the row we had when he accepted his knighthood?

SIR RICHARD: You objected to that? In heavens name why?

DESDEMONA: I don't think you'd understand, Sir Richard.

SIR RICHARD: I've never met anyone who's opposed to accepting an honour. I mean only nutters and…

DESDEMONA: You must move in a very select circle. Huntley Palmer Jones used to say that every time someone in the Labour Party accepted a title, it made him nauseous. He used to believe in the abolition of the honours system, the Lords and the monarchy. Now do you see why his accepting an honour was a total betrayal.

SIR RICHARD: Well, people change you know. You shouldn't hold that against him.

PROSECUTOR: Was that the last big row before you…

DESDEMONA: Oh, no. We argued all the time. When his government forced kids to pay tuition fees, soon after he'd joined them, we fought. In private he admitted it was a mistake. That became his regular refrain. 'I'm not saying mistakes weren't made, but…' Then he moved on to Transport and helped push through the privatisation of the air-traffic controllers. Even the Tories were opposed to that one. Another row. He defended the government's refusal to take back the railways from the gangs who prefer profit to passenger safety. Another row. Surprise is that I waited so long to execute him.

SIR RICHARD: Well exactly. I mean the railways. You've got me on that one. Even I might have been tempted to knock off John Pr…I mean…not literally you know.

DESDEMONA: (*Smiles sweetly.*) Of course not, but I understand. It's the despair, the feeling that nothing you can do will change anything. Makes one a terrorist.

SIR RICHARD: Now look here Dr Jones. Who said anything about terrorism. I mean…

DESDEMONA: Oh come, come Sir Richard. No need to get coy. I committed an act of individual terror. You thought of it… In some countries the difference between thinking it and doing it isn't that great. If the

Intelligence Services knew that you were thinking of bumping off the Prime Minister.

SIR RICHARD: The Deputy Prime Minister… I mean not that I was even thinking seriously…

DESDEMONA: Quite. But if you were thinking of it at all and mentioned it to your wife or friend and your house happened to be bugged, what was to stop an MI5 hit-man carrying out a pre-emptive strike and executing you?

SIR RICHARD: Now Dr Jones, we live in a democracy.

DESDEMONA: Exactly. And you were threatening to disrupt its functioning.

SIR RICHARD: Well, then. I could argue that by refusing to accept the desire of an overwhelming majority to bring the railways back under state control the government was ignoring the wishes of the people.

DESDEMONA: You're learning, Sir Richard. I hope before this day is over you'll have thrown your knighthood back in their face.

SIR RICHARD: Now you're going too far.

 PROSECUTOR: The last time you saw your husband, Dr Jones. What was it exactly that provoked you to murder him in cold blood?

 DESDEMONA: I appointed myself Judge, jury and executioner. Just like the United States.

PROSECUTOR: I take it you're against capital punishment.

DESDEMONA: I am, except in conditions of war, when different rules apply.

SIR RICHARD: Yes, but…

DESDEMONA: Sir Richard, haven't I said enough to convince you that this official residence had long become a war-zone. Sir Huntley and I were on different sides…

SIR RICHARD: While sharing the same bed…

DESDEMONA: You're just obsessed with sex. Aren't you getting enough of it at the moment.

SIR RICHARD: Long, long ago, my brother used to wear a badge. Make Love Not War. It would appear that you and the late Home Secretary did both.

DESDEMONA: Wrong. We slept together. But for over two years we did not make love. I lacked desire. He was otherwise occupied… A spot of lunch?

SIR RICHARD: I am feeling a bit peckish, but let's get this over with and then I might trouble you for the scrambled eggs on smoked salmon.

DESDEMONA: Smoked wild salmon. Tastes completely different from the farm-bred variety. There's a mega difference you know.

SIR RICHARD: Like old Labour and new Labour?

DESDEMONA: Not bad. But not quite there.

PROSECUTOR: The last meeting with your husband, Dr Jones?

DESDEMONA: At first it seemed like just another row, but insults were dropped like cluster bombs and then… Now it's for real, isn't it? Everything I say will be…

SIR RICHARD: Yes. So please try and be as exact as you can.

DESDEMONA: He was late that night, as usual…

As she begins to speak the scene changes to flashback mode.

Music: Brahms Violin Concerto.

Car door slamming.

Front door opens.

DESDEMONA is reading a book and munching a carrot.

Is that you?

HUNTLEY: Sorry, I'm late. Hope you didn't wait.

DESDEMONA: (*Carries on reading.*) For what?

HUNTLEY: Supper.

DESDEMONA: Should I have?

HUNTLEY: You sound pissed off…as usual.

DESDEMONA: I am.

HUNTLEY: Now look…

DESDEMONA: I don't want to look. I'm tired of looking. What I see is a monster.

HUNTLEY: (*Laughs.*) Oh I see. Jekyll becomes Hyde every evening.

DESDEMONA: You're so banal. You think in clichés. Why don't you have some supper? The whisky's on the sideboard and the hazelnuts are in the kitchen. If you're a really good boy and finish the bottle you can have some dessert. Brandy and almonds.

HUNTLEY: (*Pours a very large whisky.*) It's the same every bloody day. It's like returning to a war zone. No food in the house. You're in a sulk playing the victim. What is it today? The collapse of our health service? Or has another train gone off the rails and you've got worked up about privatisation?

DESDEMONA: (*Picking up the evening paper.*) Ophelia's school…remember. Its been sold off to a multinational. Trains for profits. Hospital for profits and now schools for profits. Hurrah for New Labour.

HUNTLEY: I always wanted her to go to Cheltenham Ladies College…she would have turned out differently. You sacrificed her education for the sake of your principles!

DESDEMONA: You mean it would have stopped her becoming a lesbian? (*Laughs hysterically.*) You poor fool. Anyway she didn't want to go there. Wanted to be with her friends.

HUNTLEY: Des, why do you go on like this at me. I'm just a friendly neighbourhood politician trying to earn a crust… Sorry. Sorry. Only joking.

DESDEMONA: You're despicable.

HUNTLEY: Why?

DESDEMONA: If you still don't understand, I give up.

HUNTLEY: Thought you already had. A long time ago. When I got the knighthood you freaked out. It had nothing to do with politics. It was for my services to English cricket and John Major proposed it…

DESDEMONA: YOU accepted it, you big black arsehole. You lost my respect then…

HUNTLEY: Meaning…

DESDEMONA: Meaning that you weren't always the sad, complacent, vegetable that you now are.

HUNTLEY: I can't bear this any more. It used to be once a year, then once every six months, then once a month, once a week and now it's every fucking day. The civil war must stop, Des. If you despise me so much why don't you leave? Can't fit in? Then fuck off!

DESDEMONA: That's what New Labour managers tell us every day.

HUNTLEY: Bloody right, too. Can't work with a constant barrage from people like you or your trade union chums. You started the war, Dessy. All I wanted was a bit of peace when I came home. I work hard you know. I am of some service to this state, even if you now find me repulsive. When times change we have to make a choice. I could have become a head-banger like some of your friends. Repeating timeless truths, subjecting Labour ministers to endless abuse, but incapable of offering any serious alternative.

DESDEMONA: You even sound like Thatcher. You began the war, Sir Huntley. Oh you were clever. Took me by surprise. I'm only joining the government to do a tiny bit of good. You know Dessy we can't have everything at once. It has to be a slow process. If at the end of the first term I've accomplished nothing, I'll get out. That's what you said. Remember? Or has whisky wiped your slate clean. Tabula rasa? And what did you accomplish? Couldn't even regulate the meat trade. Many farmers hold you responsible for the foot and mouth disease. But the resistance has begun. A new generation of trade-unionists is refusing to lie down and be steam-rollered by your corporate cronies. And I'm with them.

HUNTLEY: Regulate, control, nationalise, trades unions. That world has gone. We can't legislate socialism if the people…

DESDEMONA: The people. You mean the corporate criminals who run this world. Enron. World.Com. Anderson Accounting. There are photographs of you, not to mention your stinking leaders with all these guys.

Even the great thinker-President in the White House, up to his nose in these scandals just like his Vice President, has to admit that deregulation accelerated the rot. But you can't see that your fucking government is decomposing before your very eyes. And Iraq…Iraq. I'll never vote for you again. And the system works through fucking rogues like you…

HUNTLEY: Don't fucking swear Des. I hate that more than your politics. We seem to have reached a new stage. So now I'm venal and corrupt. You've never said that before.

DESDEMONA: I only realised today that the three company's who are trying to build you more prisons have offered to buy you a little summer retreat, a cosy little lust-nest in Tuscany. You kept that a secret.

HUNTLEY: (*Aside.*) Ever seen a black man go white? How did you find out?

DESDEMONA: The Toolbar again. They e-mailed you the details of the place. You make me sick.

HUNTLEY: I haven't accepted their offer.

DESDEMONA: But you did go and inspect the property. Where is it?

HUNTLEY: Its near Lucca. A beautiful old restored monastery in the mountains. As you lie in the bath you get a glimpse of the valley. The courtyard is just from another world. Oh Dessy you'd love that place. It was used by the fascists during the war and the trenches from where they machine-gunned the resistance are still intact.

DESDEMONA: That's nice, dear. And what would you have to do in return?

HUNTLEY: Already done it. It's a new contract to build a secure facility in Somerset for asylum seekers and illegals.

DESDEMONA: Secure facility? You mean a concentration camp, like they're doing in Australia.

HUNTLEY: Slightly exaggerated, but…

DESDEMONA: So let me get this straight. The firm that has got the franchise to build your camps is giving you a little thank-you present in the shape of a twelve-bedroomed monastery in Tuscany.

HUNTLEY: The two things are unrelated. Its just that I'm close friends now with Peter. You know we play golf together and that's how the Tuscan thing arose…

DESDEMONA: Save that for the Daily Mail…political opportunism and greed usually go together. You meet all these rich guys and want to live like them and they make it easy for you.

HUNTLEY: It's not the money.

DESDEMONA: Oh really. What is it then? Even you can't believe that this is doing any good.

HUNTLEY: You'll laugh if I tell you.

DESDEMONA: Try me.

HUNTLEY: I want to be the first black Prime Minister of Britain.

DESDEMONA: Why not marry Prince Charles and become the first black queen! (*She laughs, screams and laughs again.*) This can't be serious. You're winding me up. Get real, boy.

HUNTLEY is enraged by her response. He walks towards her as if to strike her, but controls himself. He is breathing heavily.

HUNTLEY: You want me to leave all this…

51

DESDEMONA: I never wanted all this. I wanted you. But you wanted all this and more and that's why I no longer want you. You can take your Special Adviser to the monastery in Tuscany and fuck her in the priest's hole till she's blue in the face and you're purple. Then have a bath together while you watch the sunset and plan your campaign to become Prime Minister. Perfect. Sex, politics and corruption all rolled up in a delightful Tuscan monastery. Is there a cemetery attached?

HUNTLEY: No. Why?

DESDEMONA: Just wondered.

HUNTLEY: We've reached the end Dessy. It's become unbearable, I know. You pushed me away…

DESDEMONA: I did. I wanted to marginalise you, push you to the edges of my life. It was the only way I could carry on living here.

HUNTLEY: So the blame is not all mine.

DESDEMONA: Blame? You still don't understand do you. How many deportation orders have you signed? And how many dead civilians in Basra and Baghdad will you tolerate? If you'd walked out when they invaded Iraq I would have forgiven you everything. But no. That blood-shot adjutant of the White House who occupies Number 10 flattered you into staying.

HUNTLEY: How do you know?

Screen thought: HUNTLEY and Blair socialising, body-language of flattery and servility.

DESDEMONA: Because I know what works with you. Well tonight I'm deporting you from our bedroom. Sleep in the spare room or here or the loo. Just don't come near me. (*She stalks out.*)

HUNTLEY: Goodnight, Dessy.

End Flashback.

SIR RICHARD: That wasn't the end?

DESDEMONA: No, but it wasn't far off.

SIR RICHARD: Tell me.

DESDEMONA: He couldn't sleep. Came up and tried to get into bed with me. I pushed him off and he must have come down here. At about two in the morning I heard him groaning. I came down and he pleaded for an injection to help him sleep. Wasn't an unusual request. Done it hundreds of times before. Whenever he was tense and excited. The night he accepted the knighthood. When he became a junior minister, and so on. I thought long and hard and then gave him a lethal dose.

SIR RICHARD: Detectable in an autopsy.

DESDEMONA: Virtually impossible.

SIR RICHARD: And if you were arrested, charged and tried, how would you explain yourself to the Judge and jury?

DESDEMONA: Betrayed hopes. Lost illusions. I would explain how and why New Labour sold its soul to the corporations. Correction. It never had a soul.

Flash-forward scene:

A courtroom-drama. DESDEMONA is in the dock. ANDREA ADELARD is the prosecutor, cardboard cut out jury (half the faces are black) and judge. Played out simultaneously on the screens.

PROSECUTOR: So politics is your only defence?

SIR RICHARD: I can't imagine it.

DESDEMONA: Yes, but politics isn't an abstraction, you know. It's the lives of ordinary people. People used, abused, ignored and abandoned by the politicians they have elected. The scrapheap gets bigger every day. My late husband symbolised the corruptions of power. What if the jury acquits me? Justifiable homicide. Eh?

PROSECUTOR: Dr Jones, you have already pleaded guilty to the murder of your husband. But you also plead mitigating circumstances. What gives you the right to be judge, jury and executioner?

DESDEMONA: If it is justified in this war for a state to carry out a pre-emptive strike, why is it not justified for an individual to punish the perpetrator of that war? If someone had done so in the Europe of the Thirties the world would have benefited.

PROSECUTOR: That is an outrageous suggestion m'lud. Are you now comparing fascist dictators to elected politicians…

DESDEMONA: But the principle remains exactly the same. It's like saying that it's fine if an elected politician uses chemical and nuclear weapons, but not if he isn't elected. Either the use of these is wrong in which case it applies to everyone or it's justified no matter who uses it. We can't have one law but applied differentially. That would make an ass of the law. I did what I had to do in the hope that it might deter others. I have committed a crime of political passion.

ANDREA: (*Aside.*) Fuck. She might pull it off.
(*To Judge.*) M'lud I need a recess to see if we can reach some agreement with the defendant.

DESDEMONA: I will not compromise. I want the jury to decide.

End flash forward.

SIR RICHARD: Will you excuse me for a few minutes, Dr Jones.

She leaves the room.

Sir RICHARD dials No 10.

Jonathan, its me. You heard all that? Well? Disaster I'm afraid. Every imaginable bean will be spilled in public. I think we have to move fast. Yes, of course. Is Miss Adelard in the van with you. I need to see her now. Thanks.

ANDREA enters the room.

SIR RICHARD: Ah, Miss Adelard. Come in.

ANDREA: Where's Lady Bitch?

SIR RICHARD: She's in the kitchen. Now we only have a few minutes. You've spoken to Jonathan…?

ANDREA: Yes, yes we've come to a satisfactory arrangement…

SIR RICHARD: Good, good… Er, please sit down. Right, well I've prepared a statement for you. Now let me see…yes, 'I, Andrea… etc, etc. Last night, Sir Huntley Palmer Jones rang me in the middle of the night. He'd had a row with his wife and was obviously distressed. I went round to comfort him. And after a few drinks we made love.' (*To ANDREA.*) Sex. 'Later, after returning from making coffee, I found Sir Huntley collapsed on the settee etc…called an ambulance…dead on arrival…etc.' How does that sound?

ANDREA: …The settee? May I have a look.

SIR RICHARD: Yes, yes… (*Pause.*) So, if you just… (*Producing a pen.*)

ANDREA: (*Sweetly.*) Certainly.

SIR RICHARD: Right, well…nice to see you taking it on the chin. (*As ANDREA gets up.*) Enjoy Tuscany. The monastery's in your name isn't it?

ANDREA: (*On exiting.*) Heil Huntley.

DESDEMONA enters, distracted.

 DESDEMONA: Sir Richard. Where are you?

He rushes in.

 SIR RICHARD: Just had the pathologist's report. You're in the clear.

 DESDEMONA: But I don't want to be. I want to speak to the world. I want to tell them why I had to do what I did.

 SIR RICHARD: Bon voyage, Dr Jones.

SIR RICHARD backs out of the room and exits.

DESDEMONA hums and switches on the television.

A young half-naked woman is reading the news perched on a bar-stool. It's obvious that she's reading from a cue and she smiles throughout.

TV NEWSCASTER: The Home Secretary, Sir Huntley Palmer Jones, died in the early hours of this morning after a fatal heart attack. He was taken to Westminster Hospital where all attempts to revive him failed. As the news spread, tributes poured in from the world of politics, sport and industry. Sir Huntley, the son of a Trinidadian factory worker was born in West London in 1946. He was married and had…

She switches the television off in a rage.

DESDEMONA: (*Aside.*) At least the azaleas are out…

ANDREA ADELARD enters the room in an over-excited state.

ANDREA: Desdemona. I mean, Dr Jones. The Prime Minister and the Cabinet are on their way to offer their condolences. They'll be here in half-an-hour. The whole national press wants to see you with his colleagues. Now you will be…

 DESDEMONA: (*Her face relaxes.*) The entire cabinet?

ANDREA: Yes, yes. It's fantastic. It's to show their complete solidarity with him.

DESDEMONA: I see. And they'll ALL be here at the same time.

 ANDREA: Yes.

DESDEMONA: Well that changes everything. Why don't you go to the kitchen and make some cucumber sandwiches, while I prepare a cocktail. The whole Cabinet! (*Aside.*) Are you thinking what I'm thinking?

The End.

The Stigma Manifesto

'Would the world ever had been made if its maker had been afraid of making trouble? Making life means making trouble. There's only one way of escaping trouble: and that's killing things. Cowards, you notice, are always shrieking to have troublesome people killed.'

George Bernard Shaw

'It seems to me better to represent things as they are in actual truth, rather than as they are imagined.'

Niccolo Machiavelli

1

IN these times where the word 'post' has become a universal prefix, 'irony' a form of cultural oppression and any serious political commitment is deemed vile, we need new forms of resistance. We are for real irony, Swiftian sarcasm instead of the weightless iconoclasm that masquerades as critical theatre. At a time when much energy is expended to make us believe that deep-down the world is really conflict-free and any opposition to the new order is pointless, we are delighted to be stigmatised by the enemies of light and conformists of every stripe. We're political and we're proud. Today, when, in the eyes of those who rule us, the whole of humanity have become customers, we need a dissident theatre more than we ever did in the past.

2

OUR age needs to be wrenched out of the prison of the 20th century, which ended with a broken backbone. Buds will swell again. A hundred flowers will blossom once more. Stigma will challenge the insolence, the stupidity, the clichés and cadences of contemporary politics. It will lampoon the courtiers and sycophants of the New World Order. It will target those who send the message, but also shoot the messenger. Both are guilty.

3

HOPE is an active emotion, killed by passivity. Our plays are written to prevent silence from being misinterpreted, to impede the destruction of the spirit, to encourage flame-throwers in a time when people are running out of matches, to create apprentices even though the sorcerer has run away, to defend the collective imagination.

4

STIGMA will not aim to please. The arrows of calumny and the stones of abuse will not deflect us from our aims. If more than a few London critics ever like our work, we will be duty bound to ask ourselves where we went wrong. Stigma will reach out to the parts usually ignored by contemporary culture and, for that reason, will welcome genuine feedback and criticism from those who read or see our work. The Stigma web-site is intended to be a site of debate and discussion, not self-congratulation.

5

WE shall write and perform wherever we can find the space. Form will be determined by the content. We will be happy to give the Stigma seal of approval to like-minded productions anywhere in the world. No more tear-stained eyes. No more despair. Revive the stormy spirit. Revive mockery. Revive the spirit that seeks to interrogate power rather than lie humbly in its path. Come waving hands, come exulting, come with hope in your heart. Let us laugh together.